3-Ingredient Appetizers to Wow Your Family and Guests

Easy but Elegant Appetizers That You Can Make with Just 3 Ingredients

By

Heston Brown

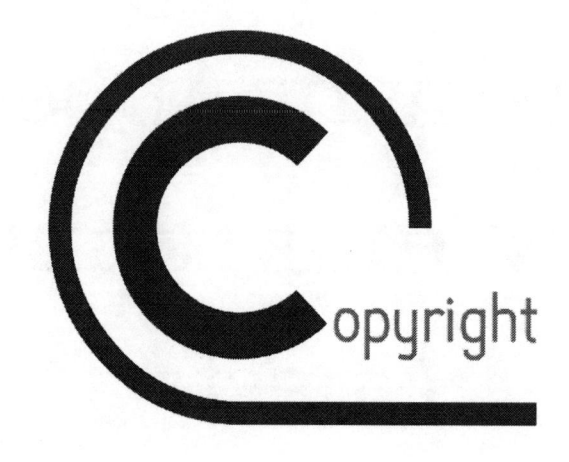

Copyright 2020 Heston Brown

All rights reserved. No part of this Book should be reproduced by any means including but not limited to: digital or mechanical copies, printed copies, scanning or photocopying unless approval is given by the Owner of the Book.

Any suggestions, guidelines or ideas in the Book are purely informative and the Author assumes no responsibility for any burden, loss, or damage caused by a misunderstanding of the information contained therein. The Reader assumes any and all risk when following information contained in the Book.

Table of Contents

Introduction 6

Recipes 8

    Barbecue Meatballs 9

    Granola Pretzel Sticks 11

    Sausage Bacon Snack 13

    Poutine 15

    Roasted Buffalo Cauliflower 17

    Chicken Drumsticks with Jalapeno and Lime 19

    Chocolate and Hazelnut Spread 21

    Frozen Banana Cereal Popsicles 23

    Piggies Ring 25

    S'more Pops 27

    Chocolate Chips 29

    Tumbleweed Sticks 31

    Peanut Butter and Jelly Skewers 33

    Lemon Bark 35

Pink Sandwich Cookies	37
Chocolate Truffles	39
Sausage and Chive Pinwheels	41
Quesadillas	43
Pecan and Caramel Candies	45
Mushroom and Bacon Bites	47
Peanut Butter Cups	49
Roasted Carrot Sticks	51
Choco-Mint Popcorn	53
Apple and Peanut Butter Sandwiches	55
Barbecued Jalapenos	57
Peanut Cookies	59
Bacon Rolls	61
Pesto Spirals	63
Baked Pumpkin Seeds	65
Potato Chip Chunks	67
Asian Cream Cheese Dip	69
Cheese with Chocolate and Black Sea Salt	71

Smoked Bacon Wraps 73

Chili Cheese Fries 75

Sugar Cookies with Pretzels 77

Pesto-Stuffed Mushrooms 79

Cheese, Ham, and Apple Wraps 81

Crispy Elephant Ears 83

Conclusion 85

About the Author 86

Author's Afterthoughts 87

Introduction

Inviting your family and friends to your house is exciting. Nevertheless, it can be pretty stressful when the date is fast approaching. You can be stressed with all the planning. With this book, you can come up with yummy 3-ingredient appetizers without putting in much work. Do you want variety in your kids' snacks? This book got you covered as well.

In no time, you can easily whip up one or more appetizers if you are able to strategize your ingredients well. Since there are only 3 ingredients in all of our recipes, we made sure that these are not only packed with flavor but are also made to be vibrant. After deciding which appetizer to make, you can serve these on a board or a platter.

Do you find it hard to believe in making something festive out of 3 ingredients? You better flip the pages now and try the recipes yourself.

Recipes

Barbecue Meatballs

This is the ideal appetizer to make at the last minute because it is very easy to follow.

Prep Time: 30 minutes

Serving Size: 20

Ingredients:

- 1 pack frozen fully cooked Angus beef meatballs
- ⅓ cup of beer
- 1 cup of barbecue sauce
- Thinly sliced jalapeno pepper (optional)

Procedure:

1. Cook the meatballs following the directions in the package.

2. Mix beer and barbecue sauce in a small saucepan.

3. Combine the meatballs alongside the mixture. Put some jalapenos on top if you want before serving.

Granola Pretzel Sticks

Aside from being convenient, these snacks are healthy, crunchy, and sweet. You will surely have fun making these. You can also substitute granola with bacon bits, nuts, or cereals.

Prep Time: 25 minutes plus standing

Serving Size: 2 dozen

Ingredients:

- 24 pretzel sticks
- 1 pack dark chocolate chips
- 1 cup of granola (no raisins)

Procedure:

1. Using a 2-cup glass measuring cup, melt chocolate chips in a microwave. Stir until it becomes smooth. In a large shallow dish, put the melted chocolate on one side.

2. Roll half of every pretzel with chocolate. Let the excess chocolate drip.

3. Sprinkle some granola onto the pretzels.

4. Set the pretzel sticks on wax paper and keep them in an airtight container.

Sausage Bacon Snack

Your guests will surely enjoy these tasty bites as finger foods or serve these with fondue. You can also eat these with an egg dish.

Prep Time: 20 minutes with chilling plus 35 minutes baking

Serving Size: Around 3 ½ dozen

Ingredients:

- 2 packs thawed frozen fully cooked breakfast sausage links
- ¾ lb. sliced bacon
- ½ cup and 2 tbsp. of packed brown sugar

Procedure:

1. Preheat the oven to 350 degrees.

2. Cut bacon slices crosswise and sausage links into two.

3. In a shallow bowl, put ½ cup of brown sugar and roll the sausage links.

4. Place a toothpick on each sausage and place them in a 15x10x1-inch baking pan lined with foil.

5. Cover and put them in your refrigerator for at least 4 hours or overnight.

6. Put one tbsp. of brown sugar. Bake the sliced bacon for 35 to 40 minutes or till it becomes crispy and turn once. Put the remaining sugar.

Poutine

These warm fries with gravy and cheese curds on top are famous in Canada. You can enjoy the traditional grease even with just frozen potatoes and packed gravy.

Prep Time: 30 minutes

Serving Size: 4

Ingredients:

- 4 cups of frozen french-fried potatoes
- ½ cup of cubed white cheddar cheese or white cheddar cheese curds
- 1 envelope of brown gravy mix
- ¼ tsp. pepper

Procedure:

1. Prepare potatoes and gravy mix following the package instructions.

2. Add some pepper.

3. Put fries on a plate, then place cheese and gravy on top.

Roasted Buffalo Cauliflower

Are you craving something savory? You better try making this healthy appetizer.

Prep Time: 25 minutes

Serving Size: 8

Ingredients:

- 1 medium head cauliflower (sliced in florets)
- ½ cup of Buffalo wing sauce
- 1 tbsp. canola oil
- Blue cheese salad dressing

Procedure:

1. Preheat the oven to 400 degrees.

2. Throw cauliflower in oil and place in a 15x10x1-inch pan.

3. Roast for 20-25 minutes or until it becomes tender and light brown. Stir once.

4. Place in a bowl and cover with Buffalo wing sauce.

5. Top with dressing before serving.

Chicken Drumsticks with Jalapeno and Lime

If you are not a fan of hot sauce in bottles, this grilled chicken recipe is great because you will create fresh pepper sauce. Everyone will love the unique kick of this recipe.

Prep Time: 25 minutes

Serving Size: 6

Ingredients:

- 12 chicken drumsticks
- 1 jar of red jalapeno pepper jelly
- ¼ cup of lime juice
- 1 tsp. salt
- ½ tsp. pepper

Procedure:

1. Heat lime juice and pepper jelly in a small saucepan on medium heat until they melt. Place a half cup of the mixture aside.

2. Put some salt and pepper on the chicken.

3. Grease your grill rack and grill the chicken on medium heat for 15 to 20 minutes or until the thermometer reaches 170 to 175 degrees. Cover and occasionally turn the chicken.

4. In the last minutes of cooking, baste the remaining lime and pepper jelly mixture.

5. You can serve with the extra mixture if there is anything left.

Chocolate and Hazelnut Spread

Even though there are a lot of chocolate-hazelnut spread varieties in groceries, there is nothing better than making your own at home. You can eat it with toast, shortbread cookies, banana chunks, and pretzels, among many others.

Prep Time: 15 minutes

Serving Size: 1 ½ cups

Ingredients:

- 2 cups of toasted hazelnuts
- 3 to 4 tbsp. baking cocoa
- 1 ¼ cup of confectioner's sugar
- A dash of salt

Procedure:

1. Put hazelnuts in a food processor. Cover and let it process for 2 to 3 minutes until the mixture pulls back from the sides of the processor.

2. Slowly add salt, cocoa, and confectioner's sugar. Continue to process until you have the consistency you like. Place it in the refrigerator afterward.

Frozen Banana Cereal Popsicles

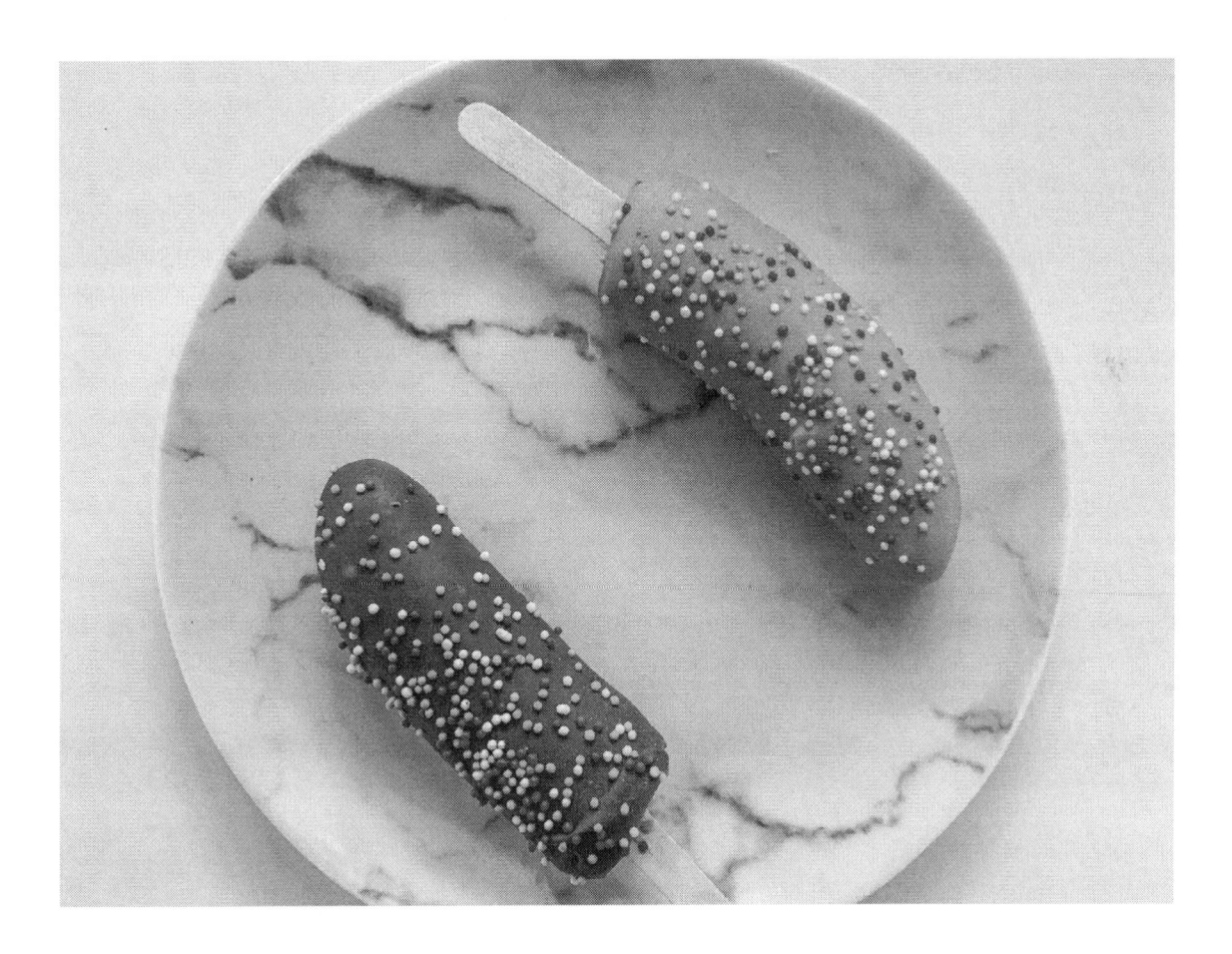

This recipe is a perfect weekend snack for your kids. You can even ask them to help you to make snacking more fun.

Prep Time: 15 minutes plus freezing

Serving Size: 8

Ingredients:

- 2 cups of Fruity Pebbles cereal
- ¾ cup of strawberry yogurt
- 4 peeled medium bananas (sliced crosswise in halves)
- 8 wooden popsicle sticks

Procedure:

1. In different shallow bowls, put cereal and yogurt.

2. Using the sliced side of bananas, place the popsicle sticks in.

3. Dunk the bananas in yogurt and coat with cereal.

4. Place the dipped bananas in baking sheets with paper and wax.

5. Freeze for an hour or until the bananas harden.

6. Place in an airtight freezer-safe container, seal, and return the popsicles to the freezer.

Piggies Ring

This beautiful piggies plate looks like a Christmas wreath when sprinkled with rosemary in the middle. This makes for a very nice appetizer for the holidays.

Prep Time: 20 minutes plus 20 minutes baking

Serving Size: 3 ½ dozen

Ingredients:

- 42 small smoked sausages
- 2 tubes of refrigerated crescent rolls
- Fresh rosemary sprigs

Procedure:

1. Preheat the oven to 350 degrees.

2. Spread out crescent rolls and divide every tube into 8 triangles. Out of the 16 triangles, cut 14 triangles lengthwise to make 3 triangles.

3. Put a sausage on the wider part of the smaller triangles and tightly roll.

4. Sort 24 appetizers by placing them with the side down in a 10-inch circle on a baking sheet lined with parchment paper. Put the remaining appetizers in the middle to create a 7-inch circle.

5. Bake for 16 to 18 minutes or until it becomes golden brown.

6. For the remaining 2 triangle doughs, make a bow and place them on a separate baking sheet. Bake for 10 to 12 minutes or until they become golden brown.

7. Let the ring cool for 5 minutes before transferring to a serving place. Put the bow at the bottom and finish off with rosemary sprigs.

S'more Pops

When your kids want to have a candy-themed party, you can serve them these pops. They are also great as gifts, bake sales, and potlucks.

Prep Time: 20 minutes

Serving Size: 2 dozen

Ingredients:

- 24 large marshmallow pieces
- 4 coarsely crushed graham crackers
- 4 oz. melted milk chocolate candy
- 24 lollipop sticks

Procedure:

1. In a shallow bowl, put crushed graham crackers.

2. Insert a lollipop stick in each marshmallow piece.

3. Coat ⅔ of every marshmallow in melted chocolate and let excess coating drip.

4. Dip in the crushed crackers covering around half of the chocolate coating.

5. Place dipped marshmallows on waxed sheets, let them set, and place them in an airtight container.

Chocolate Chips

Everyone will love the sweet and salty flavors of these appetizers. Aside from just using 3 ingredients, these can be made at the last minute. You can also use apple slices instead of potato chips.

Prep Tim: 15 minutes

Serving Size: 6

Ingredients:

- 3 cups of kettle-cooked or regular potato chips
- 1 tsp. shortening
- ½ cup of semisweet chocolate chips

Procedure:

1. Place the potato chips on a baking sheet lined with waxed paper.

2. Melt chocolate chips and shortening in a microwave. Mix until it becomes smooth.

3. Drizzle on the chips.

4. Place in the refrigerator for 5 minutes or until the chips are set.

Tumbleweed Sticks

On some roads in Texas, tumbleweeds blow. These sweet sticks will remind you of the Old West.

Prep Time: 20 minutes plus chilling

Serving Size: Around 4 dozen

Ingredients:

- 1 can of potato sticks
- 1 cup of butterscotch chips
- 1 cup of smooth peanut butter

Procedure:

1. Melt peanut butter and butterscotch chips in a large metal bowl or large microwave-safe bowl over boiling water.

2. Gradually stir potato sticks in.

3. Shape the mixture by using a rounded tablespoon. Place these on baking sheets lined with wax and paper.

4. Place in the refrigerator for 10 to 15 minutes or until they set.

Peanut Butter and Jelly Skewers

Here is a wonderful twist to the classic PBJ for new lunch ideas to make for your kids.

Prep Time: 10 minutes

Serving Size: 4 skewers

Ingredients:

- 2 peanut butter and jelly sandwiches
- 1 sliced small banana
- 1 cup of seedless green or red grapes
- 4 wooden skewers

Procedure:

1. Slice sandwiches in 1-inch squares.

2. Put a grape, sandwich square, and banana slice alternately on a skewer. Do the same for the rest of the skewers.

3. Serve at once.

Lemon Bark

This white chocolate candy is a perfect blend of creamy, tangy, and sweet. It is best served in spring, but you can enjoy this at any time of the year.

Prep Time: 10 minutes plus chilling

Serving Size: 1 ¾ lb.

Ingredients:

- 2 packs of white chocolate baking chips
- 1 cup of crushed hard lemon candies

Ingredients:

1. Put foil on a 15x10x1-inch pan and put aside.

2. Melt baking chips on a metal bowl or double broiler on slightly boiling water. Stir until it becomes smooth.

3. Add ⅔ cup of crushed lemon candies and pour them on the pan. Put the remaining crushed candies. Allow it to cool and put it in the refrigerator for around an hour or until it sets.

4. Smash gently into pieces and place them in an airtight container.

Pink Sandwich Cookies

Making these frozen sandwich cookies with pink filling is possible with just 3 ingredients.

Prep Time: 10 minutes plus freezing

Serving Size: 8 sandwich cookies

Ingredients:

- 16 chocolate wafers
- ½ cup of spreadable strawberry cream cheese
- ¼ cup of strawberry yogurt

Procedure:

1. Beat yogurt and cream cheese in a small bowl until it becomes blended.

2. Put some mixture on the bottom half of the wafers. Place the remaining wafers on top.

3. Put the wafers on a baking sheet and freeze for 30 minutes or until they become firm.

4. Serve immediately or put them back in the freezer to serve later.

Chocolate Truffles

Due to their creamy and smooth texture, chocolate truffles are considered heavenly. Nevertheless, you don't need to wait for a special occasion to serve these. All it takes is 3 ingredients to make these anytime.

Prep Time: 20 minutes plus chilling

Serving Size: Around 4 dozen

Ingredients:

- 3 cups of semisweet chocolate chips
- 1 tbsp. vanilla extract
- 1 can of sweetened condensed milk
- Coatings: espresso powder, cacao nibs, chocolate sprinkles, and Dutch-processed cocoa (optional)

Procedure:

1. Melt milk and chocolate chips in a microwave and stir until it becomes smooth.

2. Add vanilla.

3. Cover and put it in the refrigerator for 2 hours or until it becomes hard enough to roll.

4. Shape the mixture into 1-inch balls.

5. Cover with some coatings if you want.

Sausage and Chive Pinwheels

Although this appetizer is easy to make, it looks exquisite once it is served on the table. Your guests will want to try one of these because of the attention-grabbing pinwheel look.

Prep Time: 30 minutes

Serving Size: 1 dozen

Ingredients:

- ½ lb. uncooked bulk pork sausage
- 2 tbsp. minced chives
- 1 tube refrigerated crescent rolls

Procedure:

1. Preheat the oven to 375 degrees.

2. Lightly flour a surface and spread crescent rolls. Seal any openings and roll to create a 14x10-inch rectangle.

3. Within a half-inch of edges, put the sausage then place the chives.

4. Use the jelly-roll method to gently roll it. Start at the long side and press the seam to seal.

5. Slice into 12 pieces and place in an ungreased 15x10x1-inch pan an inch apart.

6. Bake for 12 to 16 minutes or until it turns golden brown or the sausage is cooked well.

Quesadillas

You can enjoy these cheesy quesadillas with salsa and sour cream or as a chili dip. This recipe is a good starter.

Prep Time: 15 minutes

Serving Size: 6

Ingredients:

- 4 warmed flour tortillas
- ½ cup of salsa
- 1 ½ cups of shredded Mexican cheese blend

Procedure:

1. On a greased baking sheet, put the tortillas.

2. Mix the salsa and cheese. Spread on half of every tortilla. Fold them afterward.

3. Broil 4 inches away from the heat for 3 minutes or until they become golden brown.

4. Slice into wedges.

PROVOKED

HOW WASHINGTON STARTED THE NEW COLD WAR WITH RUSSIA AND THE CATASTROPHE IN UKRAINE

SCOTT HORTON

Advanced Praise for *Provoked*

"*Provoked* is manna from heaven for anyone who wants to know where the extreme Russophobia in the West came from, as well as the central role the United States played in causing the Ukraine war. Horton provides a detailed account of America's foolish and dishonest behavior toward Russia in the years since the Cold War ended."

— John J. Mearsheimer, R. Wendell Harrison Distinguished Service Professor of Political Science at the University of Chicago

"Scott Horton has become an invaluable chronicler of the destruction wrought by our interventionist foreign policy. With his new book *Provoked*, Scott blows the lid off the mountains of lies used to justify Washington's waste of billions of dollars and countless Ukrainian lives in a futile proxy war with Russia. Truth is the greatest disinfectant and Scott Horton's crucial account of this awful chapter in U.S. foreign policy is like a spring cleaning. Read this book and pick up copies for your friends…and adversaries!"

— Dr. Ron Paul, former Texas congressman, chairman and founder of the Ron Paul Institute for Peace and Prosperity and co-host of *The Liberty Report*

"Scott Horton's important new book traces America's journey to war and intervention through a succession of presidencies and builds a case that points to a frightening, potential final destination for the United States: isolation and alienation from most of the world. Scott's message is simple. Stop now before it's too late."

— Col. Douglas Macgregor, U.S. Army (ret.), CEO, Our Country Our Choice

"Scott Horton is a treasure. He is also the neocons' nightmare. He knows their deceptions and lies and he is fearless in exposing the disasters they have wrought. *Provoked* is the most thoroughly researched, rationally grounded, and compellingly presented assault on war and defense of peace written in English in the post-9/11 era. It will become the standard against which all similar works are measured, and indispensable reading for all who need to understand how the American government has time and again brought civilization to a terrifying precipice."

— Judge Andrew P. Napolitano, *New York Times* best-selling author and commentator, host of the *Judging Freedom Podcast*

"Scott Horton's new book is one of the rare literary works that is impeccably sourced, unimpeachable in its logical conclusions — and fearless in presenting the truth, regardless of how unpopular or inconvenient it may be. It's a hard read, though. Not because of its length — its very thorough — but for its revelations and implications: our country has some ugly warts that must be addressed and some sins for which it must atone. If we honestly look ourselves in the mirror and make necessary changes, we can avoid some of the worst outcomes. Ignore Scott's sage observations, however, and we could be in for a rough future."

— Lt. Col. Daniel L. Davis, U.S. Army (ret.), author of *Eleventh Hour in 2020 America: How America's Foreign Policy Got Jacked Up – and How the Next Administration Can Fix It* and host of *Daniel Davis – Deep Dive*

Pecan and Caramel Candies

With a combination of sweet and salty taste, these candies surely make for the ideal light snacks. This is another great appetizer recipe you can make with your kids.

Prep Time: 5 minutes plus standing

Serving Size: 4 ½ dozen

Ingredients:

- 54 pretzels
- 54 pecan halves
- 54 Rolo candies

Procedure:

1. Preheat the oven to 250 degrees.

2. On baking sheets lined with foil, place the pretzels an inch apart. Place a Rolo candy on top of each pretzel.

3. Bake for 3 to 4 minutes or until the candies become soft. No need to worry because the Rolo candies will maintain their shape.

4. Top with pecans at once. Then, press the candy to spread into the pretzel. Let it rest until set.

Mushroom and Bacon Bites

This is an ideal appetizer for any occasion. These bites are easy to prepare; you just need to put in some barbecue sauce. If you want to make your family cookout or dinner extra special, then we definitely recommend trying this.

Prep Time: 20 minutes

Serving Size: 2 dozen

Ingredients:

- 12 halved bacon strips
- 1 cup of barbecue sauce
- 21 medium fresh mushrooms

Procedure:

1. Get a piece of bacon and wrap every mushroom. Secure each piece using a toothpick.

2. Place the mushrooms on soaked wooden or metal skewers and coat with barbecue sauce.

3. Grill without any cover on indirect medium heat for 10 to 15 minutes or until the bacon becomes crispy and the mushrooms become tender.

4. Turn and baste from time to time with the extra barbecue sauce.

Peanut Butter Cups

If you are a busy parent, you should check out this peanut butter cup recipe. It is easy, yummy, and quick. You can even bring these to the parties or bake sales.

Prep Time: 35 minutes plus 15 minutes baking

Serving Size: 3 dozen

Ingredients:

- 36 unwrapped peanut butter cups
- 1 pack peanut butter cookie mix

Procedure:

1. Preheat the oven to 350 degrees.

2. Prepare the peanut butter cookie mix following the package instructions.

3. Make 1-inch balls by rolling the dough and then place in greased small muffin cups. Evenly press the dough on the bottom and upper part of every cup.

4. Bake for 11 to 13 minutes or until it sets.

5. Right after baking, place a peanut butter cup in every cup and press gently.

6. Allow to cool for 10 minutes and remove the cups carefully.

Roasted Carrot Sticks

Do you want to have a healthier alternative to French fries? If so, then you can try these carrot sticks. You just need to pop these in the oven and serve them fries-style.

Prep Time: 20 minutes

Serving Size: 5

Ingredients:

- 1 lb. fresh carrots (sliced into half-inch sticks)
- ½ tsp. salt
- 2 tsp. olive oil

Procedure:

1. Put sliced carrots on a 15x10x1-inch baking pan.

2. Sprinkle some salt and oil and coat all the carrots.

3. Bake without a cover at 450 degrees for 10 to 12 minutes or until crispy tender.

Choco-Mint Popcorn

All your family and friends will love this as a snack or as a treat together with coffee post-dinner.

Prep Time: 20 minutes

Serving Size: 2 quarts

Ingredients:

- 8 cups of cooked popcorn
- 2 tbsp. butter
- 1 pack Junior Mints

Procedure:

1. Put the cooked popcorn in a large bowl.

2. Melt butter and mint in a small saucepan on medium-low heat and stir until the mixture becomes smooth.

3. Coat the popcorn with the mixture and toss.

4. Place on a waxed sheet and set aside until it is set.

5. Split into small pieces and put them in an airtight container.

Apple and Peanut Butter Sandwiches

This is one of the best recipes if you want your kids to help out in the kitchen. These stackers will not only let them eat more healthily but also unleash their creativity and interest in cooking.

Prep Time: 10 minutes

Serving Size: 6

Ingredients:

- 2 medium apples
- ⅓ cup of chunky peanut butter
- Fillings: miniature semisweet chocolate chips, mini M&Ms, and granola (optional)

Procedure:

1. Core and cut the apples into 6 slices crosswise.

2. Put some of the peanut butter on the slides and sprinkle with your chosen fillings.

3. Place the other apple slices on top to make stackers.

Barbecued Jalapenos

If you plan to have a barbecue party at your place, then this recipe, which is great as hot appetizer. Many will enjoy it because of the kick from the stuffed peppers.

Prep Time: 25 minutes

Serving Size: 2 dozen

Ingredients:

- 24 fresh jalapeno peppers
- 12 halved bacon strips
- ¾ lb. bulk pork sausage

Procedure:

1. Wash jalapenos. Cut a small opening on each side of the jalapenos. Take off the seeds. Rinse and dry after.

2. Cook sausage in a skillet on medium heat until it is not pink anymore. Drain afterward, then stuff the sausage into the peppers.

3. Wrap them with bacon and secure them using wet toothpicks.

4. Without a cover, grill the peppers on medium and frequently turn for around 15 minutes or until soft and when the bacon becomes crispy.

Peanut Cookies

These peanut cookies may look simply, but they are very rich in flavor. These are very easy to make because you will likely have the ingredients available in your kitchen.

Prep Time: 30 minutes

Serving Size: 2 dozen

Ingredients:

- 1 cup of smooth peanut butter
- 1 large beaten room temperature egg
- 1 cup of sugar

Procedure:

1. Combine all the ingredients in a large bowl.

2. Using a tablespoon, scoop some peanut butter to make some balls.

3. Place the balls on ungreased baking sheets and level them out using a fork.

4. Bake at 350 degrees for around 18 minutes or until set.

5. Place on wire racks to allow to cool after.

Bacon Rolls

The aroma of warm bacon is truly mouthwatering. Your visitors will come back to the table for more. Also, they are so easy and fun to make with kids.

Prep Time: 25 minutes

Serving Size: 8

Ingredients:

- 1 tube chilled crescent rolls
- 1 tsp. onion powder
- 6 cooked and crumbled bacon strips

Procedure:

1. Divide the crescent dough into 8 triangles.

2. Place 1 tbsp. of bacon aside.

3. Put excess bacon and onion powder on the dough triangles.

4. On an ungreased baking sheet, roll the dough and position the point side downwards.

5. Put the bacon strips on top.

6. Bake at 375 degrees for around 10 to 15 minutes or until they turn golden brown.

7. Serve the appetizer immediately to enjoy its warmth.

Pesto Spirals

These are great to have in the summer if you have pesto in your garden. You can also easily buy prepared pesto at your local supermarket to add flavor to these no-fuss appetizers.

Prep Time: 25 minutes

Serving Size: 12

Ingredients:

- 1 pack thawed frozen puff pastry
- ½ cup of shredded parmesan cheese
- ½ cup of prepared pesto

Procedure:

1. Preheat the oven to 400 degrees.

2. Lightly flour your surface and unfold the puff pastry sheets.

3. Roll every sheet into a 12-inch square.

4. Within ¼-inch edges, put some pesto on a pasty sheet.

5. Put some cheese and place the extra pastry on top by lightly pressing it.

6. Slice into 12 1-inch-wide strips and twist every strip 4 times.

7. Place the strips 2-inch apart on the baking sheets with parchment, then press down the ends.

8. Bake for 12 to 15 minutes or until they become golden brown. Enjoy them while warm.

Baked Pumpkin Seeds

Making this recipe is easy. To make this fun snack, you just need to empty a pumpkin, put some spices, and bake.

Prep Time: 20 minutes (50 minutes baking)

Serving Size: 2 cups

Ingredients:

- 2 cups of fresh pumpkin seeds
- 1 tsp. salt
- 3 tbsp. melted butter
- 1 tsp. Worcestershire sauce

Procedure:

1. Preheat the oven to 250 degrees.

2. Mix the seeds with the other ingredients and evenly spread on a greased 15x10x1-inch pan with foil.

3. Bake for 45 minutes and stir every now and then.

4. Increase the setting of the oven to 325 degrees and bake for around 5 minutes or until the seeds become dry and light brown.

5. Have the seeds warm or at room temperature. Allow them to cool before putting them in an airtight container.

Potato Chip Chunks

With just 3 ingredients and without baking, you will be able to enjoy these one-of-a-kind potato chip clusters. These are sweet and salty, which makes them ideal snacks for road trips and parties. Just put them in containers properly, so they won't soften or melt.

Prep Time: 15 minutes plus chilling

Serving Size: Around 3 dozen

Ingredients:

- 2 cups of coarsely crushed ridged potato chips
- 9 oz. chopped white baking chocolate
- ½ cup of chopped pecans

Procedure:

1. Melt white chocolate using a large microwave-safe bowl.

2. Add the pecans and potato chips.

3. Scoop tablespoonfuls of the mixture on waxed baking sheets lined with paper.

4. Place in the refrigerator until the chips are set.

Asian Cream Cheese Dip

Are you craving Asian cream cheese wontons? This dip recipe is almost the same, just that it's easier and faster to create. You can have it for parties or as an add-on to your Asian dishes.

Prep Time: 25 minutes

Serving Size: 6

Ingredients:

- 16 oz. softened cream cheese
- 2 cups of sweet and sour sauce
- 1 pack wonton skins
- Garnish: green onions (optional)

Procedure:

1. Preheat your oven to 400 degrees.

2. Using a cooking spray, grease a large baking sheet.

3. Create a triangle from every wonton skin by folding it in half. Then, put the triangles on the greased baking sheet in one layer.

4. Spatter the triangles with cooking spray or brush them with olive oil.

5. Bake for 8 to 10 minutes or until they become light brown and crispy.

6. After taking them off from the oven, let them cool.

7. At the bottom of a medium-sized casserole dish, put the cream cheese.

8. Place sweet and sour sauce on top and bake for 1 to 15 minutes or until the dip is well-heated.

9. Eat with wonton chips and put green onions if you want to garnish.

Cheese with Chocolate and Black Sea Salt

These appetizers can make your guests amazed. They add a twist to the appetizer table. You can even pair these with red wine.

Prep Time: 45 minutes plus standing

Serving Size: 6 ½ dozen

Ingredients:

- 8 oz. Monterey Jack cheese or aged cheddar
- Black sea salt
- 6 oz. chopped bittersweet chocolate

Procedure:

1. Cube cheese into 1/2 -inch pieces.

2. Melt chocolate in a microwave and stir until it becomes smooth.

3. Dip cubed cheese in the chocolate and let the excess drip.

4. Put them on a waxed sheet, then sprinkle with black sea salt.

5. Allow to stand until the cheese is set.

Smoked Bacon Wraps

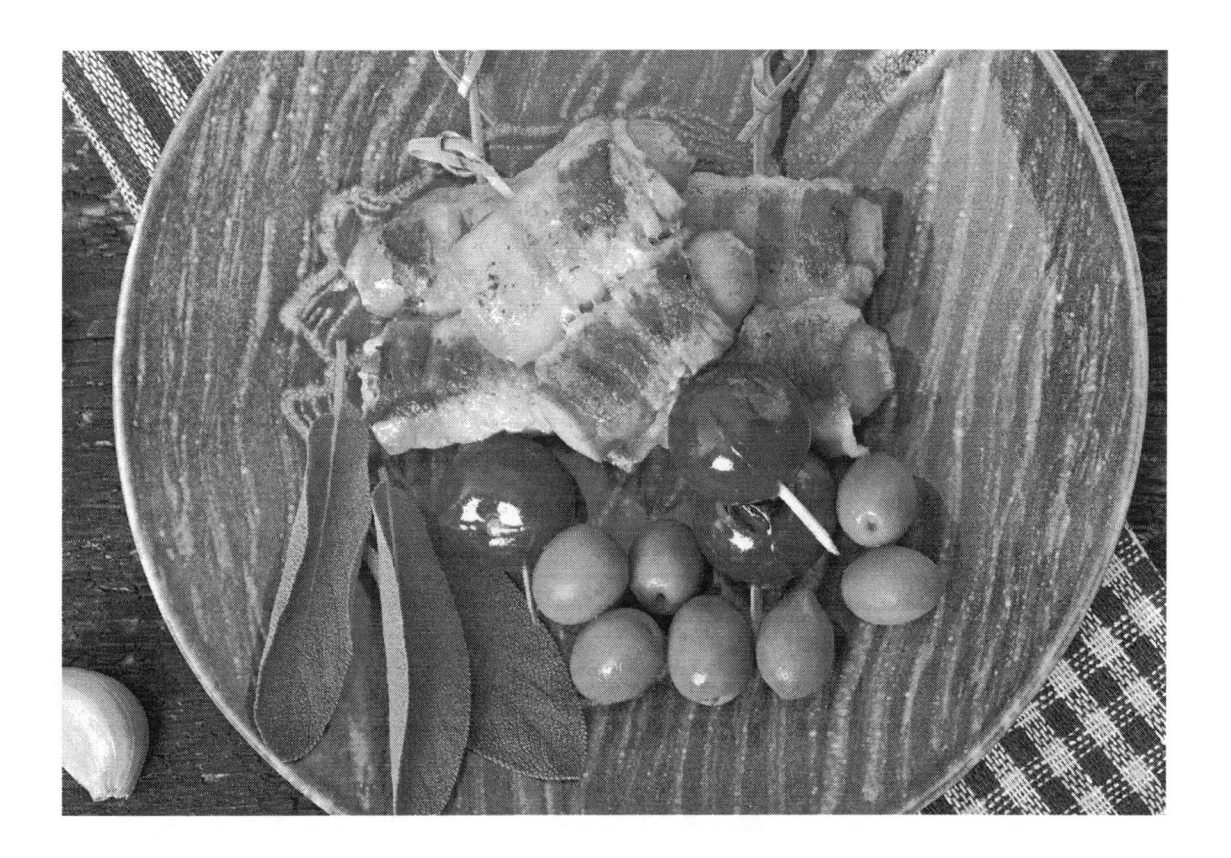

Whoever gets to try these bacon and sausage bites will surely lick their fingers. Best as an appetizer or breakfast, its combination of sweet and salty flavors makes it more fun to eat.

Prep Time: 20 minutes (30 minutes baking)

Serving Size: 3 ½ dozen

Ingredients:

- ⅓ cup of packed brown sugar
- 1 lb. sliced bacon
- 1 pack miniature smoked sausage links

Procedure:

1. Cut each bacon slice from side to side in half.

2. Wrap a bacon piece on every sausage.

3. Place the bacon-wrapped sausages in a 15x10x1-inch baking pan lined with foil. Put brown sugar.

4. Bake without cover at 400 degrees for 30 to 40 minutes or until the bacon becomes crispy and the sausage is well-heated.

Chili Cheese Fries

Chili cheese fries served at restaurants are likely packed with a lot of calories. This recipe, however, is a healthier version.

Prep Time: 30 minutes

Serving Size: 4

Ingredients:

- 5 cups of frozen seasoned curly fries
- 1 can vegetarian chili with beans
- 1 cup of shredded cheddar cheese
- 1 tbsp. olive oil
- Toppings: thinly sliced green onions, cubed avocado, and sour cream (optional)

Procedure:

1. Preheat the oven to 450 degrees.

2. Put the fries on an ungreased 15x10x1-inch baking pan.

3. Drizzle olive oil and coat the fries.

4. Bake following the package instructions.

5. Separate the fries into 4 by using baking dishes with 2 cups. Put chili and cheese on top.

6. Bake for 5 to 7 minutes or until the cheese melts.

7. Serve with toppings if you want.

Sugar Cookies with Pretzels

Since these are sweet and easy to make, you can munch on them anytime you want. With just refrigerated cookie dough, you can make these and make them even more delectable with melted white chocolate and white fudge pretzel.

Prep Time: 30 minutes

Serving Size: 4 ½ dozen

Ingredients:

- 2 ½ cups white chips or vanilla
- 2 tubes refrigerated sugar cookie dough
- 1 pack white fudge pretzels

Procedure:

1. In a large-sized bowl, crumble the cookie dough and combine 1 ½ cups chips.

2. Place tablespoonfuls of the mixture 2-inch apart on ungreased baking sheets.

3. Bake for 325 degrees for about 15 to 18 minutes or until they become light brown.

4. Push a pretzel in the middle of every cookie immediately.

5. Move to wire racks and allow to cool.

6. Melt remaining chips in a microwave and sit until smooth. Drizzle on the cookies.

Pesto-Stuffed Mushrooms

If you love Italian flavors such as pesto and mushrooms, you will surely enjoy making and eating these mushroom appetizers.

Prep Time: 20 minutes

Serving Size: 4 to 6

Ingredients:

- 1 lb. button or baby Bella mushrooms
- 1/2 cup homemade or store-bought pesto
- Garnish: toasted pine nuts and shaved parmesan (optional)
- Panko breadcrumbs (optional)

Procedure:

1. Preheat the oven to 350 degrees.

2. Remove and throw the stems of the mushrooms carefully and clean with a damp cloth to get rid of any dirt.

3. Stuff the cavity of the mushroom with half a teaspoon of pesto. If you want, you can put some Panko breadcrumbs on top.

4. Bake for 15 minutes or until the filling becomes warm and the mushrooms are cooked.

5. Garnish with toasted pine nuts and parmesan if you want.

Cheese, Ham, and Apple Wraps

The combination of the smoky flavor of the ham, sweet apples, and tangy cheese makes these wraps savory and sweet. This recipe is perfect either as lunch or a protein-packed snack.

Prep Time: 5 minutes

Serving Size: 2

Ingredients:

- 1 small Pink Lady or Granny Smith apple (cut into 8 wedges)
- 8 thinly sliced cheddar or Colby Jack cheese
- 8 thinly sliced Deli ham

Procedure:

1. On a flat surface, put a slice of ham and fold it.

2. Put a slice of cheese in the center of the sliced ham.

3. At the edge of the sliced ham, put an apple wedge.

4. Wrap the apple wedge, ham, and cheese slices.

Crispy Elephant Ears

These crispy cute treats have a classic cinnamon-sugar taste to them.

Prep Time: 20 minutes plus freezing (15 minutes baking per batch)

Serving Size: Around 2 ½ dozen

Ingredients:

- 2 tsp. ground cinnamon
- 1 pack thawed frozen puff pastry
- 1/2 cup of sugar

Procedure:

1. Preheat the oven to 375 degrees.

2. Combine cinnamon and sugar.

3. Spread a sheet of puff pastry into an 11x8-inch rectangle on a lightly floured surface.

4. Put ¼ cup of cinnamon sugar.

5. Using the jelly-rolly method, start from the short side and work toward the middle.

6. Cover with plastic, put in the freezer for 10 minutes, and do again.

7. Remove the plastic and slice the dough. Afterward, put on baking sheets that were lined with parchment.

8. Bake for 12 to 15 minutes until crispy and golden brown.

9. Transfer to wire racks and allow to cool.

Conclusion

Finally, you will surely save time and effort with the 3-ingredient appetizer recipes we mentioned above. People of all ages can also enjoy munching on these as appetizers or snacks. They are quick, yummy, and hassle-free.

What are you waiting for? Give these recipes a try now!

About the Author

Heston Brown is an accomplished chef and successful e-book author from Palo Alto California. After studying cooking at The New England Culinary Institute, Heston stopped briefly in Chicago where he was offered head chef at some of the city's most prestigious restaurants. Brown decide that he missed the rolling hills and sunny weather of California and moved back to his home state to open up his own catering company and give private cooking classes.

Heston lives in California with his beautiful wife of 18 years and his two daughters who also have aspirations to follow in their father's footsteps and pursue careers in the culinary arts. Brown is well known for his delicious fish and chicken dishes and teaches these recipes as well as many others to his students.

When Heston gave up his successful chef position in Chicago and moved back to California, a friend suggested he use the internet to share his recipes with the world and so he did! To date, Heston Brown has written over 1000 e-books that contain recipes, cooking tips, business strategies for catering companies and a self-help book he wrote from personal experience.

He claims his wife has been his inspiration throughout many of his endeavours and continues to be his partner in business as well as life. His greatest joy is having all three women in his life in the kitchen with him cooking their favourite meal while his favourite jazz music plays in the background.

Author's Afterthoughts

Thank you !!!

Thank you to all the readers who invested time and money into my book! I cherish every one of you and hope you took the same pleasure in reading it as I did in writing it.

Out of all of the books out there, you chose mine and for that I am truly grateful. It makes the effort worth it when I know my readers are enjoying my work from beginning to end.

Please take a few minutes to write an Amazon review so that others can benefit from your opinions and insight. Your review will help countless other readers make an informed choice

Thank you so much,

Heston Brown

Made in the USA
Monee, IL
12 December 2024